DYNASTY

UConn Women's Ten-Title Reign

FOUNDED IN 1764

Hartford Courant

A SPECIAL PUBLICATION

FOREWORD

For more than 250 years the Hartford Courant has had the privilege of telling Connecticut's stories — tales of triumph and tragedy, of horror and of hope.

One of those stories, one we've particularly enjoyed telling, has been the story of the University of Connecticut women's basketball team. We were there on April 2, 1995, when the team downed Tennessee to grab the school's first title. We were there for the championships — and the perfect seasons — that followed one after the other after the other after that. And we were there on April 7, 2015, when UConn captured its 10th title in 20 years.

Ten titles.

In two decades.

That's amazing. Incredible. Had we not been chronicling each win along the way in words and images, you might even say unbelievable.

But following UConn women's basketball has been as much about covering the character of a team as its athletic dominance. The women who have come through Coach Geno Auriemma's program — from Rebecca Lobo to Jen Rizzotti to Sue Bird to Diana Taurasi to Maya Moore to Breanna Stewart to the dozens of others you'll read about in this book — have shared a spirit and determination that speaks to the heart of what athletics is truly about.

We're honored to have been there every step of the way and look forward to the next chapter. Enjoy.

ANDREW S. JULIEN
Vice President / Editor • Hartford Courant Media Group

Celebrating another victory, Geno Auriemma acknowledges the crowd at the Hartford Civic Center after UConn beat UC Santa Barbara to advance to the East Regional final in 2004.
MICHAEL McANDREWS

Cover photo: Rebecca Lobo rejoices at UConn's January 1995 win over Tennessee, which put her team at No. 1 for the first time.
ALBERT DICKSON

TABLE OF CONTENTS

Hartford Courant

A TRIBUNE PUBLISHING COMPANY

Publisher and CEO: **Richard J. Daniels**
Vice President/Editor: **Andrew S. Julien**
Digital Editor: **Christine W. Taylor**

Special Projects and Publications Editor: **Naedine Hazell**
Book Editors: **Scott Powers and Nancy Schoeffler**
Writer: **John Altavilla**
Columnist: **Jeff Jacobs**
Sports Editor: **Jeff Otterbein**
Director of Photography: **Richard Messina**
Art Director: **Chris Moore**
Photo Editor: **John Woike**
Copy Editing: **Hugh Owen and Jay Spiegel**

Photographers: **Paula Bronstein, Tom Brown,
Jay L. Clendenin, Bradley Clift, Albert Dickson,
Stephen Dunn, Bettina Hansen, Brad Horrigan,
Michael Kodas, John Long, Bob MacDonnell,
Michael McAndrews, Richard Messina, Mark Mirko, Sherry
Peters, Cloe Poisson, Patrick Raycraft,
Shana Sureck and John Woike**

Published by Pediment Publishing, a division of the Pediment Group, Inc.
www.pediment.com. Printed in Canada.

**Capping their 2010
championship season,
President Barack Obama
honors the UConn women's
basketball team in the East
Room of the White House.**
BETTINA HANSEN

The Architects

COACHES: GENO AURIEMMA AND CHRIS DAILEY

They have been side by side for 30 years, brought together in 1985, intrigued initially by each other's ambition, personality and vision.

Geno Auriemma, the coach. Chris Dailey, the assistant. They moved into tiny offices in UConn's Greer Field House, with rotary phones and no-frills furniture. This is where they talked and plotted and hatched the plan to transform a program no one paid attention to, that had won 36 games in the previous four seasons, into something no one will forget.

Geno Auriemma, here with Shea Ralph after the victory over LSU in the 2000 East Regional Final, wears his emotions on his sleeve.

Coaches Shea Ralph, Chris Dailey and Marisa Moseley get a little kooky before an event saluting the 2010 Final Four teams.

And the thing was, they both assumed it would be a starter home.

"What was I thinking? Four years max," Auriemma said.

But Pat Meiser, the former UConn administrator and University of Hartford athletic director who headed the search committee to replace Jean Balthaser, saw something special immediately.

"During the summer and fall preceding their first season, the preparation was very intense," Meiser said. "You could tell they knew exactly what they wanted

to do, both in terms of image, messaging, visibility and attitude. They were very serious about building a program."

Good things began to happen, more quickly than either expected. There was an unexpected trip to New Orleans for the Final Four in 1991. UConn lost, but things were moving in the right direction.

"Oh, I'm sure Pat may have thought we had a plan, but I'm not exactly sure we knew exactly what it was," said Dailey, now the associate head coach. "For us, the plan was try to do things a certain way, the way we knew it would

have to be done to be successful."

The more Auriemma and Dailey got to know each other — and others got to know them — it became clear they were perfectly matched, yet different. Checks and balances — it isn't just about branches of government. It works for people, too.

He was a brilliant coach who enjoyed doing things she did not. She was a brilliant coach and didn't mind taking on the tasks he didn't like. Auriemma's spontaneity, certainly in public, was matched by Dailey's matter-of-factness.

"Chris has such a presence in our program that I would venture to say it's probably more significant and more impactful than a majority of head coaches have on their own program," Auriemma said. "We would not be where we are, and I would not be where I am without what Chris has done for me and our program."

Most important, she was, and will be forever, the one in charge of writing Auriemma's version of "Pygmalion." The players who came to her, Eliza Doolittles in their own ways, were her responsibility to mold.

Dailey made sure they walked the kind of walk necessary to turn them into ladies of high basketball society, ones who would be respected not only for their command of the game, but for their comportment.

The UConn women's program does not allow exposed tattoos. Its players must stand when being interviewed and wear no headphones when walking in public. And no makeup, nail polish or jewelry on the basketball floor during the season. Its players do not engage in social media during the season.

"It's the system," Rutgers coach C. Vivian Stringer said. "They do a masterful job of putting people into a system. And the system is

Many times, Chris Dailey provides the firm hand that keeps Geno Auriemma from a technical foul, but on this occasion, the damage is already done.

excellent. Frankly, I didn't know that it would sustain as long as it has, but what's true about UConn is true about any good operation. You find the players you can coach and teach them to play your style in your system."

UConn women's basketball is not a team or program as much as it has become a national brand. Blow your nose, you reach for Kleenex. Raise a daughter who loves basketball, you reach for UConn. And for those who have chased the Huskies over the past three decades, they have become an aspiration and a destination.

"I remember Geno telling me, 'Look, we'll go from last to the middle, and then we'll go somewhere that we'll be really good and be able to win the national championship,'" Dailey said. "I said, 'How hard could it be to go from the bottom to the middle?'

"I knew we didn't want to be a one-hit wonder after 1991. And then you don't want to win just one; you continue to work, you want to be viewed as a program, not just a team that went to a Final Four."

UConn has produced players who have become the sport's icons, collegiate and WNBA champions, Olympic gold medalists, Hall of Famers.

Auriemma and Dailey have won 10 national championships in 20 years, twice winning three in a row. And in the summer of

STEPHEN DUNN

The rosters change from year to year, but Geno Auriemma remains at the hub of the program's success, having been to 16 Final Fours.

2016, with Dailey's help and with many of their players by his side, Auriemma will try to win a second Olympic gold medal.

They have written history by being dedicated to principles and goals.

The numbers are staggering: 16 Final Four appearances, including eight straight; 22 consecutive trips to the Sweet 16; 20 30-win seasons; five unbeaten seasons; a record 90-game winning streak; and a 10-0 record in national championship games. Auriemma's winning percentage (917-134, 87.25) is the

greatest in the game's history. The program produced 12 Olympians and never lost a game in the American Athletic Conference.

"Sometimes it's natural to take it for granted," Auriemma said. "You need to realize if it was that easy, then a lot of other people would have done it. It's not easy. We do certain things to put ourselves into position to win.

"I want my players to know it's not just because we are Connecticut and have the best players. The NCAA isn't just going to hand us things because we've been there so many times. We have to earn it every year. And every team I've had [that has won] has earned it.

"I don't even know what to say at times. When people trot out some of the numbers describing the things we've done ... I am sometimes kind of in awe of it myself."

Geno and Chris, the most dynamic power couple in the history of the game. And this is their story times 10.

Over the years, Chris Dailey, right, has found the secret to being both an authority figure and a trusted confidant to players such as Sue Bird, left, and Paige Sauer.

JAY L. CLENDENIN

Having done this well over 100 times, Geno Auriemma enjoys a certain security factor when he and his staff enter the arena for an NCAA Tournament game in 2010.

Under the bright lights, as he so often is, Geno Auriemma hoists the UConn women's ninth championship trophy at Gampel Pavilion.

1994-1995 SEASON: 35-0

1995 NCAA TOURNAMENT: UConn 105, Maine 75 • UConn 91, Virginia Tech 45 • **Sweet 16:** UConn 87, Alabama 56 •
Elite Eight: UConn 67, Virginia 63 • **Semifinal:** UConn 87, Stanford 60 • **Final:** UConn 70, Tennessee 64

The Start Of Something Big

T en years into a job he originally figured wouldn't last more than four, Geno Auriemma approached the 1994-95 season knowing that the window of opportunity to win his first national championship — the window he had stared through since losing to Virginia in the 1991 national semifinals — was closing fast. Rebecca Lobo, his transcendent senior center, would graduate after the season.

Auriemma thought he had had a chance to win the year before, overcoming early-season road losses at Stanford and Seton Hall to win 21 straight heading into an Elite Eight match with North Carolina in Piscataway, N.J. Oh well, Tar Heels by 12. See you next year.

And so Auriemma and associate coach Chris Dailey decided to run a new scheme, one that relied on motion and was called the triangle

Geno Auriemma has taken Connecticut fans on an incredible ride — 10 national titles and five undefeated seasons — that started when the Huskies went 35-0 in 1995.
BRAD CLIFT

ROSTER: Carla Berube, Kim Better, Jamelle Elliott, Jill Gelfenbien, Kelley Hunt, Rebecca Lobo, Sarah Northway, Jennifer Rizzotti, Missy Rose, Brenda Marquis, Nykesha Sales, Pam Webber, Kara Wolters
COACHES: Geno Auriemma, Chris Dailey, Meghan Pattyson, Tonya Cardoza

Rebecca Lobo and the Huskies set out to unseat
Dana Johnson and No. 1 Tennessee. Playing
with a splint on her broken pinkie, Lobo had 13
points, eight rebounds and five blocks in a 77-66
win on Jan. 16, 1995.
ALBERT DICKSON

The dorm room shared by seniors Pam Webber, far left, and Rebecca Lobo isn't much more than a place to hang your hat – and boots. In 1995, Lobo was the player of the year and an Academic All-American.

SHANA SURECK

offense, to take advantage of their players' skills. They tried it out on a European exhibition tour in the summer.

"I told the kids that if we learned anything on our European trip, it's that we can't concern ourselves with who we play or what they're going to do," Auriemma said. "The bottom line in being a successful team is how good you are at doing the things you do and, secondarily, how good you are at preventing someone from doing what they want to do."

As it would turn out, UConn became pretty good at doing just that.

So it began on Nov. 26, 1994, with an 80-point win against Morgan State, one partially fueled by junior point guard Jen Rizzotti, who shook off back spasms that had sidelined her 10 days earlier.

When Auriemma went to

UConn comes through the Big East wars unscathed, relying on its stars but also on role players including senior guard Pam Webber (32), above, against Syracuse, and junior forward Jamelle Elliott (33), left, against Miami – both of whom started every game. Elliott averaged 10.9 points and 8.1 rebounds for the season.

Jennifer Rizzotti nudges past
Villanova's Sue Glenning in the
regular season finale on Feb. 27,
a game in which she scored her
1,000th career point.

STEPHEN DUNN

The Huskies have to scramble a little in a 97-87 win over No. 17 Kansas, part of a made-for-CBS double bill with the men's teams on Jan. 28 before 17,000 at Kemper Arena in Kansas City.

Rizzotti's home in New Fairfield a few years earlier on a recruiting visit, Connecticut's 1992 high school player of the year prepared the Italian immigrant a Japanese dish she'd been introduced to during her family's four-year stay in Japan.

"I knew then," Auriemma said, "that she was going to do things on her own terms."

The Huskies followed the Morgan State win with 11 more, including a 23-point road thumping of Kay Yow's NC State team on Dec. 10. The Big East rivals that followed routinely fell by large

The Huskies know they're good, but slaying Tennessee for the first time astonishes even Rebecca Lobo, left. Her season averages: 17.1 points, 9.8 rebounds, 3.7 assists and 3.5 blocks. Opposite: Kim Better, left, and Jennifer Rizzotti, right, celebrate at crowded Seton Hall, where UConn subdues the Pirates 85-49 for the Big East Tournament title, led by MVP Kara Wolters, center, who scored 32 points.

ALBERT DICKSON

STEPHEN DUNN

At left, Pitt fouls Nykesha Sales, one way to stop the Big East rookie of the year, who hit 43.2 percent of her threes. Above: Kara Wolters, right, against Villanova gives UConn a 6-foot-7 presence in the post.

margins — including Providence and Seton Hall, which lost by a combined 98 points. UConn was ranked second heading into a Monday afternoon game, Jan. 16, 1995, at Gampel Pavilion against No. 1 Tennessee on ESPN.

Auriemma's world — the world of women's basketball — was about to change. With Gampel jammed, Rizzotti's three-pointer delivered the crushing blow as the Huskies beat the Lady Vols 77-66 to become No. 1.

Two weeks later, the Huskies improved to 17-0 with a 10-point win at Kansas, as Lobo scored 25 points with 12 rebounds in 36 minutes. Soon after, the Huskies started showing up on national news shows and in the major newspapers across the nation. They had everyone's attention.

All they needed was the national championship.

They won the Big East Tournament after finishing their first unbeaten season (18-0) in the conference. Maine, Virginia Tech and Alabama fell in the first three rounds of the NCAA Tournament before another meeting with Virginia, the place Auriemma had worked as an assistant, in the Elite Eight. Though they trailed by seven at the half, the first time they were down at intermission all season, the Huskies won, 67-63.

The next day, Auriemma and Lobo found out just how closely people had been watching when they were chosen as Naismith coach and player of the year.

All that was left was the Final Four in Minneapolis. Kara Wolters, the 6-7 center, scored 31 to help

the Huskies to a 27-point win over Stanford, with iconic coach Tara VanDerveer. Fittingly, Tennessee awaited.

VanDerveer stoked the flame after the game by saying that UConn had no chance to beat Tennessee again in the final.

Not a chance? Despite a 38-32 halftime deficit, despite foul trouble that ended Lobo's day with 4:52 to play, baskets by Jamelle Elliott and Rizzotti gave UConn the lead late in the second half. The Huskies won 70-64 to finish the season 35-0 and earn their first title.

"The last entry in my journal will say, 'We're national champions, and you better believe it because it's true,' " Lobo said back then. "We're 35-0 and have done something, and there's not a single person who can take that away from us."

The nets, the trophy, the T-shirts —
these can only point to one thing: The
Huskies have beaten Tennessee at
the Target Center in Minneapolis to
capture their first NCAA title.

PAULA BRONSTEIN

Their championship credentials now fully vetted, the Huskies – including Carla Berube, driver's side, and Kara Wolters – parade through Hartford on April 29 , a great chance to connect with their fans.

SHANA SURECK

BACK2BASK
BIG EAST
194
CONNECTICUT 50   CONNECTICUT 32   199
UCONN WOMEN'S
BASKETBALL

CARLA BERUBE
KARA WOLTERS

1999-2000 SEASON: 36-1

2000 NCAA TOURNAMENT: UConn 116, Hampton 45 • UConn 83, Clemson 45 • **Sweet 16:** UConn 102, Oklahoma 80 •
Elite Eight: UConn 86, LSU 71 • **Semifinal:** UConn 89, Penn State 67 • **Final:** UConn 71, Tennessee 52

Dominance Begins

How to say this politely? Let's try putting it this way: The enduring impact of UConn's first national championship was not exactly what you might have expected.

Oh, there was certainly much to discuss; Jen Rizzotti, Nykesha Sales and Kara Wolters completed All-America seasons and moved on to pro careers.

There was also an endless wave of momentum. The Huskies won four Big East Tournaments, winning 130 of 143 games while their faithful, in love unconditionally, dutifully formed long ticket lines outside the Hartford Civic Center.

But the era from 1996-1999 was also a comparative dark age for a program that would eventually become the brand name of its sport.

After losing in the national semifinals to Tennessee in 1996, the Huskies spent the next three seasons faltering in big spots, twice in the Elite Eight and then in the Sweet 16.

SHERRY PETERS

ROSTER: Svetlana Abrosimova, Sue Bird, Swin Cash, Marci Czel, Stacy Hansmeyer, Kennitra Johnson, Asjha Jones, Shea Ralph, Christine Rigby, Paige Sauer, Kelly Schumacher, Keirsten Walters, Tamika Williams
COACHES: Geno Auriemma, Chris Dailey, Tonya Cardoza, Jamelle Elliott

Desolate after a Sweet 16 casualty against Iowa State in 1999, opposite, the Huskies make it back to the Final Four in 2000 with a victory over LSU, a joyous moment for Christine Rigby (44), Stacy Hansmeyer (20) and Paige Sauer.
MICHAEL McANDREWS

After a disappointing end to their freshman seasons, Tamika Williams (34) and Swin Cash come back determined to write a different script.

JAY L. CLENDENIN

Tamika Williams, then a sophomore, keeps her composure when surrounded by Lions in the national semifinal.

Pumping in 17 points, Shea Ralph leads UConn to a 68-62 win over Kentucky.

So before the 1999-2000 season began, coach Geno Auriemma and his players needed to take a deep breath.

Swin Cash — one of the four top recruits brought in the year before, along with Sue Bird, Asjha Jones and Tamika Williams — taped a picture to her locker of herself crying after the 1999 Iowa State loss.

"We all know what we want to do this year," Cash said in August. "We all want to make sure it doesn't end like it did" the previous season.

With his talented sophomore class beginning to emerge, Auriemma made tactical lineup changes, taking minutes away from seniors Paige Sauer and Stacy Hansmeyer so others, including veteran defensive specialists like center Kelly Schumacher, could play.

The two seniors did not complain. So beloved by fans was the Oklahoman Hansmeyer —

UConn's season tips off in Big Ten country, where the Hawkeyes miss their first 20 shots, and Sue Bird & Co. win, 73-45.

JAY L. CLENDENIN

The Big Dance brings Hampton University to Storrs, but the Pirates pose no danger to Swin Cash or the Huskies, trailing by 49 at the half.

nicknamed Bam-Bam — that she would sing the national anthem on Senior Night.

The chemistry seemed ripe for another run.

"We can't wait to get out there," said junior Shea Ralph. "This season started the day last season ended."

And the Huskies played like it, starting with a win over Iowa and losing only once in the regular season, to Tennessee on Feb. 2 at the Civic Center, when Semeka Randall hit two clutch shots for the Lady Vols in the final 30 seconds.

After another 16-0 roll in the Big East and an uneventful run to the tournament championship, UConn beat Hampton, Clemson, Oklahoma and LSU to send Auriemma home to Philadelphia for the Final Four. After UConn beat Penn State in

The pressure, in this case from BC's Alissa Murphy, rarely gets to Svetlana Abrosimova, the team's leading rebounder (6.2) and second-leading scorer (13.4) behind fellow first-team All-American Shea Ralph (14.3).

There's no escaping this time, as Sue Bird is guarded by Kristen Clement and Michelle Snow (00) in a 72-71 loss to Tennessee on Feb. 2, 2000 at Gampel — UConn's only defeat.

SHERRY PETERS

Tamika Catchings, above, gets a little more altitude than Svetlana Abrosimova for one of her 13 rebounds. The AP player of the year, Catchings scored 19 points in the 72-71 game, Feb. 2.

In another game, Jan. 8, Kelly Schumacher, below and the Huskies put the squeeze on Kyra Elzy and the Lady Vols in the first meeting of the season, a 74-67 UConn win in Knoxville.

One look at Paige Sauer, above, says it all. Tennessee outscored the Huskies 44-37 in the second half of the Feb. 2 game.

Tamika Williams, below, has a big game for UConn with 19 points in 25 minutes, but the Vols don't let her beat them.

MICHAEL McANDREWS

the semifinals, he led a party bus tour that ended up at a place called Finnegan's Wake the night before the title game with Tennessee. Perhaps he had a premonition?

And what a game that was: The Huskies led by 13 at halftime, took advantage of 26 turnovers, ran the back door to perfection and won their second title, 71-52.

Ralph, voted along with Svetlana Abrosimova to the All-American team, was also most outstanding player of the Final Four, one of four Huskies on the all-tournament team.

But in the title game, it was Schumacher, a quiet Canadian who would become a professional beach volleyball player and model after a long WNBA career, who best justified the confidence her coach showed in her. She blocked

nine shots. She set an aggressive offensive tone from the start. At the other end she blocked Kara Lawson, prompting Tennessee coach Pat Summitt to call a timeout. Schumacher then made sweeping blocks on Randall and Tamika Catchings on consecutive

shots that Cash and Bird converted for baskets.

"The blocked shots definitely broke our spirit," Summitt said.

And then, in the handshake line, Tennessee assistant Al Brown angered Auriemma so with his halfhearted handshake

In the championship game, Tennessee's condition worsened because of a severe blockage, the result of a steady diet of Kelly Schumacher swats. She had nine blocks, and the Huskies followed Geno's orders for an easy win.

RICHARD MESSINA

With the victory well in hand, there's a moment to enjoy one another's company. From left, Kelly Schumacher, Sue Bird, Swin Cash, Tamika Williams, Svetlana Abrosimova, Asjha Jones, Shea Ralph and Chris Dailey. Below, it didn't take much to get a reaction out of Shea Ralph, one of the team's emotional leaders. She scored 15 in the title game on 7-for-8 shooting.

and passing glance that Geno nearly threw a punch. If not for the restraint of trusted assistant/ bodyguard Chris Dailey, Auriemma might have slugged him.

Animosity with Tennessee? It was only beginning.

"I've told these kids all year long that every pass we make in practice, every cut, every rebound, pretend like it's the one that's going to win the national championship," Auriemma said. "These kids have practiced like this all year long, and the night that they had to do it, they did better than any other time this season."

Watching the game that night from the stands was a precocious UConn recruit from Chino, Calif., a guard named Diana Taurasi. In a few years, that high school phenom would be responsible for more fun in Connecticut.

3

2001-2002 SEASON: 39-0

The Stars Come Out

T o understand the brightness that would eventually break through, one must comprehend how dense and dreary the fog was that enveloped Storrs on the morning of March 31, 2001.

    The 2000-01 season had been wonderful to that point, despite road losses to Notre Dame and Tennessee that came three weeks apart in January and February.

And it was so despite the loss of seniors Svetlana Abrosimova to a foot injury in February and Shea Ralph to one final knee injury during the Big East Tournament.

Despite the absence of their All-America pivot points, the Huskies rolled through another unbeaten conference season and four comparatively uneventful 2001 NCAA Tournament games to meet Notre Dame in the national

Opposite page, the starting five – Swin Cash, Asjha Jones, Sue Bird, Diana Taurasi and Tamika Williams – had no weakness. Right, the four seniors and one central sophomore listen to late-game instructions in the Elite Eight.

JAY L. CLENDENIN

MICHAEL McANDREWS

ROSTER: Ashley Battle, Sue Bird, Swin Cash, Maria Conlon, Asjha Jones, Stacey Marron, Jessica Moore, Diana Taurasi, Ashley Valley, Morgan Valley, Tamika Williams
COACHES: Geno Auriemma, Chris Dailey, Tonya Cardoza, Jamelle Elliott

semifinals at the Savvis Center in St. Louis on March 30.

At the half, UConn led, 49-37. At the end, Notre Dame won by 15. Freshman Diana Taurasi was 1-for-15 from the field, 0-for-11 from three. A 27-point swing.

"I don't think I've ever seen our team as focused and ready to play as we were in that whole first half," UConn coach Geno Auriemma said. "And then it all fell apart in the second half."

But here's the thing about UConn: It has always had stars to brighten the sky. And as the next season approached, it was clear the Huskies finally had their first real constellation.

Had any team in the history of women's basketball had seniors as diverse and dynamic as Sue Bird, Asjha Jones, Tamika Williams and Swin Cash? And a sophomore as fearless as Taurasi?

"They have everything," said Nancy Lieberman, the basketball Hall of Famer. "It's the best starting five I've ever seen."

When Auriemma peered through his telescope before the

The games were usually one-sided, but a little arm-twisting was needed at times, as shown by Jessica Moore against North Carolina, above left, and Tamika Williams against Vanderbilt in the preseason WNIT.

The calls didn't always go the Huskies' way, and such situations could require a little restraint on Diana Taurasi's part, above, or a synchronized attack from Geno Auriemma and Chris Dailey.

A 40-16 rampage in the second half turns the NCAA second-round game with Iowa into an 86-48 laugher.

In the regionals in Milwaukee, above right, Penn State boasts high-scoring Kelly Mazzante, but UConn answers with Sue Bird, who has 24 points and six assists, then 26 and 11 against Old Dominion. Left, Swin Cash and Asjha Jones all but topple a Monarch.

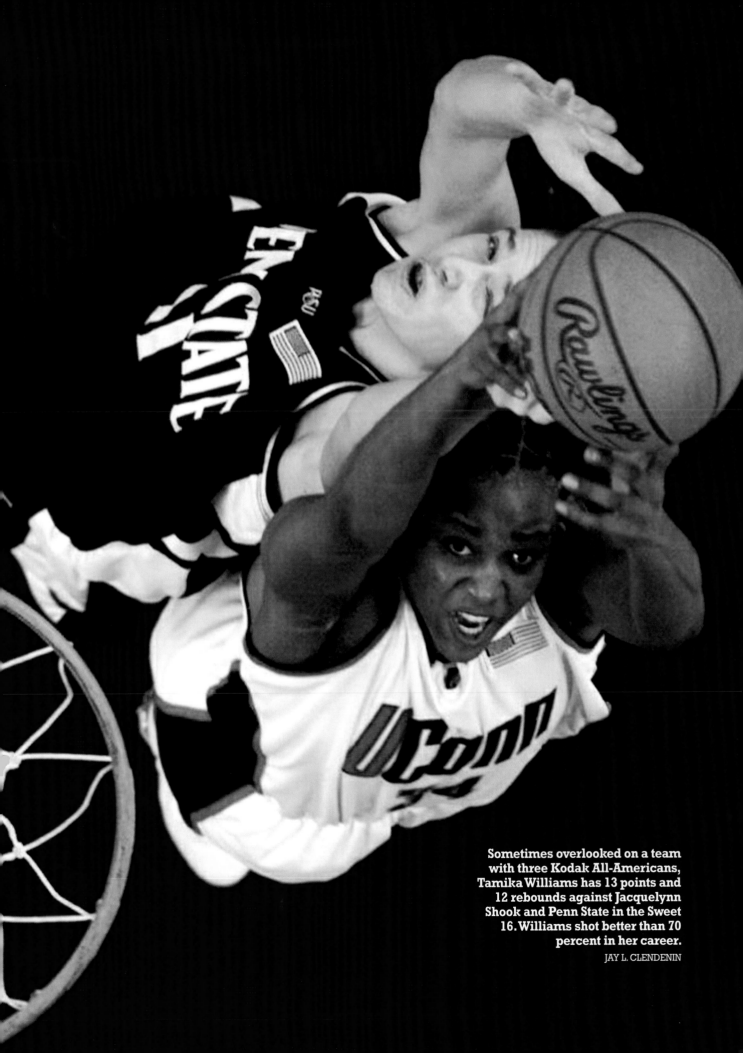

Sometimes overlooked on a team with three Kodak All-Americans, Tamika Williams has 13 points and 12 rebounds against Jacquelynn Shook and Penn State in the Sweet 16. Williams shot better than 70 percent in her career.

JAY L. CLENDENIN

At the Final Four in San Antonio, Swin Cash finds herself in a tight spot against two hardworking Volunteers — Michelle Snow, left, and Tasha Butts.

The postgame produces some light moments for, left to right, Jessica Moore, Maria Conlon and Ashley Battle, after the 79-56 win over Tennessee, but soon it was time to focus on Oklahoma.

season, it wasn't hard for him to see those stars aligning in the shape of a third championship trophy. Yes, that was the Big Dipper he wanted to sip his Barolo from.

From an opening 43-point win over Fairfield, it was clear this team meant business. The skill sets that defined UConn's stars meshed into a juggernaut that recorded 30 consecutive wins — only one, at Virginia Tech on a cold January day, by fewer than 10 points.

"That's a pro team," Vanderbilt coach Jim Foster said after the Commodores fell by 19 in November. "They're ready for March."

The Huskies rolled through the Big East Tournament with lopsided wins over Seton Hall, Villanova and Boston. The NCAA

It's hardly a case of scraping by, as Sue Bird (18 points, five assists, four steals) helps the Huskies to a 79-56 over Tennessee in the semifinals in 2002.

Tournament began with victories over St. Francis (Pa.) and Iowa at Gampel Pavilion before moving on to Milwaukee where Penn State and Old Dominion fell.

That brought the Huskies, now 37-0, to the Final Four at the Alamodome in San Antonio.

Waiting in the semifinals was Tennessee. The Huskies were two victories from going 39-0, equaling the best season in Division I history, Tennessee in 1998.

You want a team? Read all about it: UConn set the NCAA single-season record for assists with 811. Its average margin of victory was 36.4 points. All five starters averaged more than 10 points, but none averaged more than 15.

"The media is setting us up for a fall," said Bird, the Associated Press player of the year, winner of the Wade Trophy and member of the 10-player Kodak All-America first team along with Cash and Taurasi.

During the regular season, the teams played Jan. 5 at Tennessee, a battle acted out before the largest crowd (24,611) to attend a women's

Asjha Jones comes armed for this one, with 18 points and 10 rebounds, in the semifinal against Tennessee.

Diana Taurasi and Tennessee's Brittany Jackson give mega-effort for a ball on the loose.

A driving force in the championship game, Swin Cash scores 20 points and grabs 13 rebounds, earning Final Four most outstanding player honors. The senior led the balanced Huskies in scoring (14.9) and rebounding (8.6).

JAY L. CLENDENIN

college basketball game. The Huskies won by 14. Taurasi had a career-high 32 points on 11-for-16 shooting.

"There is a big gap between No. 1 and No. 2," Tennessee coach Pat Summitt said. "We're all chasing Connecticut right now."

That was never more evident than when they met in the Final Four. With assertiveness that immediately knocked Tennessee off-kilter, with 18 points from Bird and Jones, 17 points and 10 rebounds from Taurasi, the Huskies rolled to a 79-56 victory.

Until the pressure relented in the final minutes when Auriemma offered his stars their curtain calls, UConn even threatened to hand Tennessee the most lopsided loss in its history, surpassing Texas' 31-point victory over the Lady Vols

The jubilation of Jessica Moore, Maria Conlon and Ashley Battle, left to right above, means the Huskies will hang another championship banner, as they defeat the Sooners, 82-70. Left, Diana Taurasi shoots over Stacey Dales, a play that drew the fifth foul on the Oklahoma standout.

JOHN WOIKE

in 1984.

All that was left was Oklahoma, coached by the pugnacious Sherri Coale, the high school coach of Stacey Hansmeyer, a senior on UConn's 2000 national championship team.

The Sooners, led by Stacey Dales, now an analyst for the NFL Network, advanced to their first title game with a victory over Duke. UConn had already defeated Oklahoma 86-72 at the Civic Center on Dec. 22.

"If people believe the championship game was played between UConn and Tennessee, they're wrong," Coale said.

Turns out, she was wrong. With five players scoring in double figures, led by Cash's 20 points and 13 rebounds, and despite

JAY L. CLENDENIN

shooting 0-for-9 on three-pointers and committing 21 turnovers, the Huskies completed their second undefeated season with an 82-70 win.

The greatest season in the history of the game was complete. Its greatest team proved powerful enough to lift a fog.

"There never was a barometer for greatness," Foster said. "Now there is: The WNBA. UConn is playing with five first-round draft choices. I don't think there's ever been a men's or women's team that can make that statement."

One week later, Bird (1), Cash (2), Jones (4) and Williams (6) were gobbled up by WNBA teams in the first round, leaving Taurasi behind to make more history.

She soon would.

JAY L. CLENDENIN

Geno Auriemma gives his seal of approval to UConn fans at the Alamodome, top. His roster is about to change dramatically: Diana Taurasi (3) will be back, but player of the year Sue Bird is among four seniors departing.

2002-2003 SEASON: 37-1

2003 NCAA TOURNAMENT: UConn 91, Boston University 44 • UConn 81, TCU 66 • **Sweet 16:** UConn 70, Boston College 49 •
Elite Eight: UConn 73, Purdue 64 • **Semifinals:** UConn 71, Texas 69 • **Final:** UConn 73, Tennessee 68

New Cast,
Worthy Encore

I t's human nature to assume that some things will never be as perfect as they once were. Consider a Yankees fan. It was hard to envision that DiMaggio would follow The Babe, Mantle would replace DiMaggio or that Munson would take over for Yogi.

But it happens. In fact, it happens almost all the time if you pay attention to history. Disney endearingly refers to this as the circle of life.

At UConn, the dread of its fan base was palpable when four of its greatest players graduated simultaneously following the 2002 national championship. Doubt reverberated like a cellphone shrilling in a quiet chapel: "How could life possibly go on without Sue Bird, Swin Cash, Asjha Jones and Tamika Williams to lead us?"

But that summer of 2002 likely was when the fundamental nature of what UConn had become kicked in. This program was no longer a one- or two-year wonder.

Needing complementary talent for Diana Taurasi, the Huskies found out that Maria Conlon could really play.

JAY L. CLENDENIN

ROSTER: Ashley Battle, Maria Conlon, Willnett Crockett, Stacey Marron, Jessica Moore, Ann Strother, Diana Taurasi, Barbara Turner, Ashley Valley, Morgan Valley, Nicole Wolff
COACHES: Geno Auriemma, Chris Dailey, Tonya Cardoza, Jamelle Elliott

A no-senior group had to come
together in the 2002-03 season, and
players including Jessica Moore, left,
and Ashley Battle moved to the forefront.
BOB MacDONNELL

STEPHEN DUNN

Considered a player with a bright future, Ann Strother quickly put her all-around abilities on display, averaging 10.1 points per game.

MICHAEL KODAS

Freshman Willnett Crockett will not be denied a rebound in a 77-59 February victory over Notre Dame in which she scored 12 points.

JOHN WOIKE

Diana Taurasi gives her blessing to a play by newcomer Barbara Turner, who led the team in scoring six times as a freshman.

This is as close as it gets for Geno Auriemma and Pat Summitt, a one-point overtime game in Hartford on Jan. 4.

Fans flock to Hartford knowing that a 55th straight win, against Georgetown, will supplant Louisiana Tech at the top of the chart. The Huskies win 72-49.

The Huskies were being built to last through an ever-expanding geographical recruiting base that began with Shea Ralph (North Carolina), Stacy Hansmeyer (Oklahoma) and Paige Sauer (Nevada) in the late 1990s.

And so, beginning with its 85-39 win over Wright State in the fall of 2002, Geno Auriemma began reassembling his program around its next fulcrum, irrepressible sophomore Diana Taurasi from California.

Meanwhile, Maria Conlon, the former Connecticut high school player of the year, the one with the UConn flag hanging off the family house in Derby, had hardly played in her first two seasons.

Still, she caught Auriemma's eye; assertive, stubborn, a hard worker, much like himself. But she also irritated him. He thought her somewhat needy, always searching for positive reinforcement.

Before her junior year, Conlon dropped some weight and most of her eagerness for validation.

And with Jessica Moore, Ashley Battle and freshmen Willnett

Nicole Wolff, left, despite a foot injury, celebrates with Willnett Crockett (23) and Barbara Turner (33), when Diana Taurasi's three-pointer forces overtime against Tennessee.

Barbara Turner, left, and Ashley Battle rub shoulders with greatness on this day, as Diana Taurasi hits a 60-footer against Tennessee at the buzzer.
MICHAEL McANDREWS

MICHAEL McANDREWS

Crockett, Ann Strother and Barbara Turner, who scored 26 in a big win over Notre Dame in February, this team quickly took off.

On Jan. 4 at the Hartford Civic Center, Taurasi hit a half-court bomb and then a jumper to send the game with Tennessee to overtime. UConn won, 63-62.

On Jan. 18 against Georgetown in Hartford, the Huskies won their 55th consecutive game, surpassing Louisiana Tech's record winning streak of 54.

"It feels good to finally break it," said Taurasi, who had 22 points and eight rebounds. "To go down in history as the only team to win that many games in a row, that goes to show how much work the coaches put in to prepare us."

The winning steak continued

MICHAEL McANDREWS

The cheery UConn contingent is ready to cap off the Big East Tournament at Rutgers with a win over Villanova, but the 52-48 loss — and the end of a 70-game winning streak — are something Ashley Battle, at top, and the Huskies hadn't seen coming.

BOB MacDONNELL

BOB MacDONNELL

NCAA Tournament games against Texas Christian, above, and Purdue, above right, weren't the easiest, but now they are affectionately remembered.

through the unbeaten regular season and stood at 70 until it ended with the Big East Tournament championship game loss to Villanova. UConn had not been beaten since its loss to Notre Dame in the semifinal of the 2001 Final Four. It had also defeated the Wildcats by 20 at home on Jan. 29 and had won its last 18 against them. But UConn's 52-48 loss also featured its fewest points in 11 seasons.

"I guess if we had been able to win 88 in a row, that would have excited me," Auriemma said. "Then we would be talking about the UCLA men's record. We would have been talking about the longest streak in all of college basketball."

The NCAA Tournament was not a breeze, either. In the second round, Texas Christian led 35-33 at the half but Taurasi's 35 points fueled an 81-66 win. The Huskies beat Purdue in the Elite Eight despite going scoreless for nearly nine minutes at the end of the

In the semifinals in Atlanta, Jamie Carey and Texas threaten to deny Geno Auriemma his 500th win, but Maria Conlon helps reject that idea.

MICHAEL McANDREWS

game.

In the Final Four at the Georgia Dome, the Huskies barely beat Texas, 71-69, in the semifinal despite being pushed around by Longhorn forward Stacy Stephens until Crockett helped turn things around in the last three minutes.

And then, before dealing with the Lady Vols again in the championship, Auriemma had a premonition. Before the game, prompted by a friendly exchange with Journal Inquirer columnist Randy Smith, Auriemma walked into the locker room and wrote the names of the previous year's starters on the blackboard.

This was his way to illustrate that there was history to respect, reputations to uphold, a responsibility to preserve continuity.

And that's what they did. Taurasi scored 28 points. Strother added 17. Conlon had 11 points, six assists and no turnovers. In fact, Conlon had only one turnover in 77 Final Four minutes.

Taurasi, the consensus national player of the year, finished the NCAA Tournament with 157 points, third-most in Division I history, and had 54 in the Final Four, fourth all-time. She was the obvious choice for Final Four most outstanding player.

Soon after, the team was in Washington to meet President George W. Bush for the second time in two years. The previous spring, the president had mispronounced Auriemma, uttering something more like, "Are-eee-mah."

"Whatever the hell the guy's name is, he can really coach," Bush said.

This time, Bush walked in saying, "Where's Geno?"

Where's Geno? Auriemma was where he had grown accustomed to being. He was on top.

"I think you told me you would be back," the president said.

"I did, didn't I," Geno replied.

BOB MacDONNELL

Brittany Jackson (25) is assessed an offensive foul in the second half of the championship game, a call that gets a charge out of Willnett Crocket. In a 73-68 win, the Huskies never trailed.

MICHAEL McANDREWS

After scoring 17 against Tennessee, freshman Ann Strother, right, joins Diana Taurasi on the Final Four all-tournament team.

BOB MacDONNELL

Played straight up by Shyra Ely, Barbara Turner contributes to the offense, scoring 10 points on 5-for-7 shooting.

After an Olympian effort in the NCAA Tournament, Diana Taurasi, right, grabs the gold, an uplifting experience for Ashley Battle, left, and the Huskies. Taurasi scored 17.9 points per game overall; 26.2 in the Big Dance.

BOB MacDONNELL

2003-2004 SEASON: 31-4

2004 NCAA TOURNAMENT: UConn 91, Penn 55 • UConn 79, Auburn 53 • **Sweet 16:** UConn 63, UCSB 55 •
Elite Eight: UConn 66, Penn State 49 • **Semifinals:** UConn 67, Minnesota 58 • **Finals:** UConn 70, Tennessee 61

Dynamo Taurasi

From the moment Geno Auriemma first saw Diana Taurasi on a basketball court, it was clear this charismatic dynamo defied simple description.

The All-American kid from Chino, Calif., was a chemical reaction, talent bubbling over the top of the beaker. But it wasn't just her ability, although it's not every day that a kid scores 3,047 points in high school. It was her attitude: confident, spontaneous, fearless. Not only was she a step ahead of the field, she also was a one-liner ahead.

Taurasi could have gone to UCLA to play close to home. But enamored of Auriemma's straight talk – she hated disingenuous recruiters – she chose UConn, embracing the enormous challenges he placed at her feet over the comfort and safety of a more familiar future.

"I probably wouldn't get a ring somewhere else," Taurasi said. "Anyone who is a player and loves basketball wants to win. And to

At Senior Night in 2004, Diana, Mario and Liliana Taurasi and Geno Auriemma know they are nearing the end of a pretty nice arrangement.

JOHN WOIKE

ROSTER: Ashley Battle, Maria Conlon, Willnett Crockett, Stacey Marron, Jessica Moore, Kiana Robinson, Liz Sherwood, Ann Strother, Diana Taurasi, Barbara Turner, Ashley Valley, Morgan Valley, Nicole Wolff
COACHES: Geno Auriemma, Chris Dailey, Tonya Cardoza, Jamelle Elliott

It wasn't her first choice, but No. 3 was a good fit for Diana Taurasi: She left Storrs as a three-time national champion and three-time Kodak All-American.
MICHAEL McANDREWS

Handed some stinging defeats, Geno Auriemma and his Huskies couldn't forget that basketball is supposed to be enjoyable.

win a national championship, that's worth more than any points that you can score."

So it was no surprise when Taurasi immediately began to engage and delight UConn fans at the Phoenix/WBCA All-America Game at the Hartford Civic Center in April 2000. With the most valuable player trophy tucked under her arm, Taurasi boldly led 7,562 fans through the U-C-O-N-N cheer and then got on a plane to Atlanta to receive the Naismith Trophy for high school player of the year.

"It just came out," Taurasi said.

She originally asked Auriemma if she could wear No. 00. When he scoffed, she asked for No. 1. He refused that, too, but he offered No. 3. Auriemma, the baseball fan, knew what the implication was — he felt she could be the Babe Ruth of women's basketball.

As a high school All-American, Diana Taurasi gives Connecticut fans a preview of her inimitable style.

First a stress fracture, then a knee injury — Nicole Wolff couldn't catch a break, playing only 13 games in her first two seasons.

It's hard to believe this could happen, but Ann Strother (43) and the Huskies allow Duke to rally from 17 down for a 68-67 win on Jan. 3, 2004.

Credit Auriemma with the second called shot in sports history, because that's exactly who Taurasi turned out to be.

Still, 2003-04, the last lap for Taurasi, Maria Conlon and Morgan Valley, did not go as smoothly as the year before. Redshirt freshman Nicole Wolff, who sat out most of her first year with a stress fracture, was lost for the season with a knee injury. Taurasi had a sore back just painful enough to be annoying.

The team won its first eight games, but then lost four — the first against Duke on Jan. 3, 2004, at the Civic Center. UConn led the Blue Devils by 17 at the half and by 12 with five minutes to play, but Duke scored 30 of the final 41 points.

Taurasi finally hit a jumper to give UConn a 67-65 lead, only to watch a sophomore from Australia, Jessica Foley, hit a three at the buzzer to end the Huskies' streak of 69 consecutive home wins, which at the time was tied with Tennessee for longest in NCAA

Becoming the first nonleague team ever to beat UConn in Hartford is a heap of fun for Mistie Bass, left, and the Duke Blue Devils.

Division I women's history. The loss also marked the first time an Auriemma team at UConn lost after leading by 20 (35-15 with 1:11 left in the half).

On Jan. 13 at Notre Dame, the Irish, unranked with six losses, beat the Huskies by 15 before a crowd of 8,574 that stormed the

court. Notre Dame ended UConn's 35-game road winning streak and became the first unranked team to beat UConn since Boston College in 1999 — a streak of 121 games.

On Feb. 28, the Huskies lost to Villanova, the team that had ended their 70-game winning streak the season before in the Big East

In a Big East semifinal tangle with Boston College, one bounce here or there could have been the difference for the Huskies, but the Eagles moved on.

MICHAEL McANDREWS

Tournament championship game. This time Israeli guard Liad Suez, who scored 21 of her 23 points in the second half, scored four in the final minute to seal a 59-56 win, spoiling the day Taurasi became the fifth UConn player to reach 2,000 points.

But the season's low point came with a 73-70 loss to Boston College in the semifinal of the Big East Tournament in Hartford, snapping a streak of 10 consecutive appearances in the conference championship game. This was not good for many reasons, mostly because the Eagles managed to shoot a tournament-record

MICHAEL McANDREWS

Chris Dailey, left, Geno Auriemma and Tonya Cardoza share frustration over the 73-70 loss to Boston College.

Barbara Turner, right, scores 25 and
Diana Taurasi gets her 2,000th career
point, but Liad Suez and Villanova
won't be pushed around.
JOHN WOIKE

One Husky is clearly out of bounds, while the other hopes to get the timeout before landing there in the East Regional against UC Santa Barbara.

Willnett Crockett, right, isn't sure what to make of reserve Liz Sherwood's shot against Auburn, while Jessica Moore is suspended in animation.

Fans in Bridgeport, above, mark another UConn milestone, and the icing on the cake is a 79-53 NCAA second-round victory over Auburn.

Janel McCarville and Shannon Schonrock, right, help Minnesota pull close in a national semifinal, but a three by Ann Strother would spark UConn's finishing kick.

63 percent against a program defiantly defensive about how it played defense.

"Anytime somebody makes a shot, it's a function of two things," Auriemma said. "You executed pretty well and the defense didn't react accordingly."

For the second season in a row, the Huskies did not win the Big East Tournament.

They needed to get their act together.

The NCAA Tournament began in Bridgeport with a win over Penn and a drubbing of Auburn in the second round to celebrate Auriemma's 50th birthday. Conlon and Ann Strother each chipped in four three-pointers. In Hartford for the East Regional finals, the Huskies beat UC Santa Barbara, with 6-foot-8 center Lindsay Taylor, and then Penn State to give themselves a shot at a third consecutive national championship.

Meanwhile, the UConn men were on their own magical run, and on April 3 in San Antonio they knocked off Duke in the national semifinals. The next night in New Orleans, Taurasi scored 18 to lead the Huskies over a Minnesota team with future WNBA players Lindsay Whalen and Janel McCarville.

And then the crescendo: The UConn men won their second national championship, defeating Georgia Tech 82-73, setting the stage for the women to complete the first sweep of NCAA basketball titles in history.

There was no way Taurasi would let it end any other way. She scored 17 points in 37 minutes in a 70-61 victory against Tennessee, taking the women to their third straight national championship.

Then she added an exclamation point: Taurasi put the ball in her hands for the last time as a Husky and punted it toward the ceiling of the New Orleans Arena.

Impetuous as ever.

BOB MacDONNELL

Diana Taurasi ends her UConn career by partying in New Orleans, while Pat Summitt absorbs a fourth NCAA title-game loss to the Huskies.

BOB MacDONNELL

For Jessica Moore, left, and Barbara Turner, nothing beats the feeling of a championship — one Moore helped deliver with 14 points and nine rebounds against Tennessee.

MICHAEL McANDREWS

2008-2009 SEASON: 39-0

2009 NCAA TOURNAMENT: UConn 104, Vermont 65 • UConn 87, Florida 59 • **Sweet 16:** UConn 77, Cal 53 •
Elite Eight: UConn 83, Arizona State 64 • **Semifinals:** UConn 83, Stanford 64 • **Final:** UConn 76, Louisville 54

Return To Splendor

B y the time Diana Taurasi got to Phoenix and the WNBA in the spring of 2004, aficionados of women's basketball, not to mention White House date-planners, had come to expect certain things from UConn.

From 1995 to 2004, the Huskies played in seven Final Fours and won each of the five national championship games they played, including three in a row from 2002 to 2004. To some this constituted a trend, to others the birth of the sport's new monarchy.

Seldom did anyone talk about women's basketball without eventually mentioning the Huskies, the impact of their stars or the frequently cheeky, mostly jokey tone of Geno Auriemma, the sport's Quotemaster General.

Yes, if only life were as simple as muscle memory, the Huskies would have sailed through their first four seasons without Taurasi

During a rare dry period after the 2004 title, Geno Auriemma was itching to coach another championship team. It would take the triumvirate, opposite, of Tina Charles (31), Renee Montgomery (20) and Maya Moore to help make it happen.

JOHN WOIKE

ROSTER: Heather Buck, Tina Charles, Lorin Dixon, Caroline Doty, Jacquie Fernandes, Meghan Gardler, Kalana Greene, Tiffany Hayes, Cassie Kerns, Jessica McCormack, Kaili McLaren, Renee Montgomery, Maya Moore, Tahirah Williams
COACHES: Geno Auriemma, Chris Dailey, Jamelle Elliott, Shea Ralph

Barbara Turner, a scrappy forward who won titles her first two seasons, saw it slip away in 2005. In 2006 she became the fifth UConn player to have 1,600 points and 700 rebounds.

Read it and weep: Renee Montgomery, center, checks the scoreboard after the OT loss to Duke in 2006. It was the last game for seniors Ann Strother, left, and Barbara Turner.

Ketia Swanier and the Huskies couldn't push past Stanford in the 2005 Regional Semifinals, losing 76-59. UConn lost eight games that season and failed to win the Big East regular season title for the first time since 1993.

Rutgers fans go to the tape, expressing displeasure with Auriemma, after he called them "ignorant" in February 2007.

as seamlessly as they had when she was around.

But it wasn't that way. A mighty rain fell on the parade.

The Huskies lost eight games in 2004-05, the most since 1992-93, when they lost 11. UConn was eliminated in the Sweet 16 by Stanford.

In 2005-06, while welcoming bright-eyed point guard Renee Montgomery, a five-loss season was punctuated by a 23-point beating in December by North Carolina. That year ended in the errant hands of Auriemma annoyance Charde Houston, in the final seconds and desolation of an overtime loss to Duke in Bridgeport in the Elite Eight.

The following year, despite the addition of freshman center Tina Charles, the Huskies lost four more, including the Big East championship game at home to Rutgers, and were bounced by LSU in Fresno in the Elite Eight.

And even in 2007-08, bolstered by the arrival of Maya Moore, a team that lost only once, by two points to Rutgers, then lost in the national semifinals to Stanford beneath the leaky roof of St. Pete Times Forum in Tampa.

UConn's Tina Charles drives to the hoop for the first score of a regular season game in February 2009 against Notre Dame.

UConn's Kalana Greene finds room between two DePaul players at a January 2009 game at Gampel Pavilion in Storrs.

Four years, 19 losses, one Final Four and no national championships. This was a kingdom under attack. All hail Baylor (2005), Maryland (2006) and Tennessee times two (2007 and 2008). Would the Huskies ever head back to the Rose Garden?

As it turned out, they would lose a big player but not another game for a very long time.

In June, the team was stunned by the departure of freshman Elena Delle Donne, the nation's best high school player. Considered the greatest young player of her generation, even when compared with Taurasi and Moore, she chose UConn — but abruptly left to play at Delaware, closer to home.

Even without Delle Donne,

High school player of the year Elena Delle Donne (blue UConn shirt) shared a laugh with fellow recruits. From left, Heather Buck, Kerri Shields, Delle Donne and Tiffany Hayes during First Night in 2007, where everybody was pumped. Delle Donne committed but would never play for the Huskies, another deflating blow to the Blue and White.

Despite protests from Pat Summitt and Tennessee, UConn was able to scoop up Maya Moore, who would become its greatest player since Diana Taurasi. She was a four-time AP first team All-American.

JOHN WOIKE

Members of the North Carolina student body, above, try to put a spell on UConn on Jan. 19. What the wordsmiths really needed was an "L" for "Loss." The No. 1 Huskies handed the No. 2 Tar Heels a 30-point loss.

The season's lowpoint came at the XL Center on Jan. 17 when Caroline Doty crashed to the floor. Geno Auriemma and trainers would later learn she had another ACL injury and would miss the rest of the season.

MICHAEL McANDREWS

the Huskies' core was incredibly hearty: four graduated seniors were replaced by three freshmen, 6-foot-3 center Heather Buck — Connecticut's high school player of the year — and guards Caroline Doty and Tiffany Hayes.

Charles, by this time a junior, was coming off a strong sophomore season and finally in tune with her coach.

But this would be Moore's team. As a freshman, she was Big East player of the year and Associated Press first-team All-American. She was just 17 points shy of becoming the program's all-time leading single-season scorer.

"You will see a more composed player on offense," Moore said. "There are times when I tried to do things too quickly, and that created turnovers. I'll take my time more this year, make strong, solid decisions."

The Huskies soared immediately, gaining steam with a memorable 28-point win over No. 4 Oklahoma on Nov. 30. Montgomery, now a senior, scored 30 with 13 assists. Moore added 27 points, 12 rebounds. And Doty was 6-for-6 on three-pointers to account for all 18

As a junior, Tina Charles, below, averaged 16.5 points, but it was her defense that likely frustrated Oklahoma's Courtney Paris. Charles had a career-high 35 steals in 2008-09. At right, UConn's Renee Montgomery is fouled as she is double-teamed by Louisville Cardinals in the 2009 finals at the Scottrade Center in downtown St. Louis.

It's not a stretch to say the game is over when Tina Charles, center, and fellow starters Tiffany Hayes, left, and Maya Moore are on the sideline. The Huskies emptied the bench in the 75-36 Big East championship game victory over Louisville.
CLOE POISSON

points.

"I told Geno after the game that if he plays like that and shoots like that, he might win the men's national championship," Oklahoma coach Sherri Coale said.

All was going well until Jan. 17, 2009, when the Huskies played Syracuse in Hartford.

Moore scored 40 that day — the most since Nykesha Sales had 46 against Stanford in 1997 and the most ever by a UConn player at home. She also surpassed 1,000 career points faster than anyone in program history and set a UConn record with 10 three-pointers in a 107-53 victory.

But Doty, who tore her left ACL in high school, injured the same knee late in the first half after scoring 17 points. She had another ACL injury and was out for the season.

Even that could not stop UConn. Two days later, with sophomore Lorin Dixon, a former high school teammate of Charles, now at the point, they crushed No. 2 North Carolina in Chapel Hill.

UConn completed the regular season 30-0 and cruised to a Big East Tournament title with a resounding 39-point win over upstart Louisville and Angel McCoughtry, the Big East player of the year in 2007. When Moore left the game with less than nine minutes to play, she had 28 points, the Cardinals just 27.

The NCAA Tournament simply was a coronation — a reaffirmation, really — featuring six lopsided wins that concluded with a 76-54 win over Louisville.

The drought was over. The Huskies completed their third undefeated championship season — the fifth in women's basketball history. Moore would be national player of the year, Charles and Montgomery joining her as All-Americans.

"Now we can breathe," said Montgomery.

MICHAEL McANDREWS

Maya Moore, top, was head and shoulders above Louisville as the Huskies waltzed to a 76-54 victory in the NCAA title game. At left, Renee Montgomery and fans at a welcome home rally at Bradley Airport in April 2009.

JOHN WOIKE

Geno Auriemma exults after netting UConn's sixth national title – and third perfect season – with the defeat of Louisville on April 7, 2009, in St. Louis.
MICHAEL McANDREWS

2009-2010 SEASON: 39-0

2010 NCAA TOURNAMENT: UConn 95, Southern (La.) 39 • UConn 90, Temple 36 • **Sweet 16:** UConn 74, Iowa State 36 •
Elite Eight: UConn 90, Florida State 50 • **Semifinal:** UConn 70, Baylor 50 • **Final:** UConn 53, Stanford 47

Perfection Yet Again

Y ou know how life is. Something might occur at any point from blueprint to bouquet that could blow the most carefully conceived plan off the table and into the trash.

Imagine how difficult it already had been for Geno Auriemma to distract fate three times and keep his teams on the left side of the score and the right side of history.

Unbeaten in 1995. Unbeaten in 2002. Unbeaten in 2009.

"It doesn't matter what the score is," Auriemma once said. "My players are always under the impression that they are going to win. I've seen teams that accept losing say, 'It's not our day today; we'll get it tomorrow.' Well, my guys refuse to accept that. They will not accept it."

If there is a level beyond perfection, UConn's intention was to stamp its logo on it in 2009-10,

Twelve days after the title game, Lorin Dixon, left, Tiffany Hayes, with cap, and assistant coach Marisa Moseley are still riding high at the victory parade in Hartford.

JOHN WOIKE

ROSTER: Heather Buck, Tina Charles, Lorin Dixon, Caroline Doty, Kelly Faris, Jacquie Fernandes, Meghan Gardler, Kalana Greene, Tiffany Hayes, Kaili McLaren, Maya Moore
COACHES: Geno Auriemma, Chris Dailey, Shea Ralph, Marisa Moseley

Could Maya Moore and the Huskies deliver again on the biggest stage? With a 53-47 win over Stanford in San Antonio, it's mission accomplished.

BETTINA HANSEN

Freshman Kelly Faris (34) seems to thrive in precarious situations. For the year she had 82 assists, 48 steals and only 44 turnovers.

following the 39-0 perfection of 2008-09, when the Huskies won every game by at least 10 points, the only team in NCAA history to do so.

"The motivation is another championship," senior Kalana Greene said. "We don't feel like life is complete now that we've won one. We still want another one."

The new ascent began without point guard Lorin Dixon, who strained her hamstring before the season. But sophomores Tiffany Hayes and Caroline Doty were there, and so was the team's only freshman, a thin but steel-plated guard from Indiana named Kelly Faris.

The Huskies also had their All-Americans, junior Maya Moore and senior Tina Charles. And nobody else did.

As Greene predicted in the fall, the team found a new level, crushing opponents, even sturdy ones like Stanford (80-68) and North Carolina (88-47). In one particularly prophetic 48-hour

period in January, Notre Dame and Duke went down by a combined 57 points.

Not only was UConn teasing improbability — a second consecutive unbeaten season — but Charles was simultaneously pursuing program scoring and rebounding records held by Nykesha Sales and Rebecca Lobo.

Charles surpassed both within minutes on the same day, during a

76-51 win at Notre Dame on March 1. UConn's 69th consecutive win by double figures capped its eighth unbeaten regular season in the Big East.

With 13:13 remaining, Charles grabbed the fifth of her eight rebounds, the 1,269th of her career, breaking Lobo's record, which had stood since 1995. And then with 4:21 remaining, Charles' basket off a missed free throw by Hayes broke

JOHN WOIKE

STEPHEN DUNN

Guards Caroline Doty, far left, and Tiffany Hayes worked well in tandem to support the Huskies. Maya Moore, center photo, and Tina Charles, above, were each a national player of the year.

CLOE POISSON

CLOE POISSON

Kalana Greene, above, makes No. 2 Stanford take notice in an 80-68 win Dec. 23, and Caroline Doty (5), above left, helps slay No. 7 North Carolina 88-47 on Jan. 9. It's no wonder fans of the No. 1 Huskies have swelled heads when ESPN's "GameDay" visits Storrs on Jan. 16 for a 70-46 win over No. 3 Notre Dame.

MICHAEL McANDREWS

Sales' scoring record (2,178), which had stood since 1998.

"It's a great accomplishment after everything I had to go through to learn how to play hard, to learn what Coach wanted from me, and to accept that's what I should want from myself on a consistent basis," Charles said. "He took me to levels I never thought I would experience."

More historic moments soon followed. UConn's 59-44 win over Notre Dame in the Big East semifinals was its 71st in a row, breaking its NCAA Division I record of 70 that Villanova snapped in the Big East Tournament championship game in 2003.

After winning the 2010 Big East

Tina Charles, opposite page, is so happy she could scream on March 1 in South Bend — a 76-51 victory in which she became the program's career leader in points and rebounds.

RICHARD MESSINA

After a 70-50 win over Baylor in the national semifinals, associate head coach Chris Dailey goes right down the line in offering congratulations to, from left, Caroline Doty, Maya Moore and Tiffany Hayes. Moore and Tina Charles combined for 55 points.

BETTINA HANSEN

A winning streak long under construction reaches a record 71 as Tiffany Hayes, below right, and the Huskies push their way past Notre Dame in the Big East semifinals in Hartford. Kalana Greene, below left, is the MVP with 15 points and 12 rebounds in the final, a rout of West Virginia.

In a long-anticipated matchup with 6-foot-8 freshman Brittney Griner (42), Caroline Doty and the Huskies force the Bears to play from behind.

BETTINA HANSEN

BETTINA HANSEN

Lorin Dixon (30) isn't letting Iowa State stand in the way of an Elite Eight berth. UConn won 74-36 in Dayton.

Tournament, the Huskies won their first four NCAA games by a combined 188 points. Counting the Big East Tournament, UConn had allowed an average of just 39.7 points in the postseason, holding all opponents to 50 points or fewer.

"It's something that I have a hard time explaining," Auriemma said. "There is nothing I could say that would make any sense. The cynic out there is saying, 'Well, everyone else must be pretty bad.' Well, I know that's not true."

In the national semifinal in San Antonio, the Huskies faced the intimidation of the game's towering shot-blocker, Baylor's Brittney Griner. Hayes drove right at her for the game's first basket 15

BETTINA HANSEN

The UConn regulars have a bench that's pulling for them. From left, Heather Buck, Jacquie Fernandes and Meghan Gardler.

A 12-point first half in the title game is difficult for all concerned, especially coach Geno Auriemma. But behind 23 points and 11 rebounds from Maya Moore, UConn takes it away from Kayla Pedersen (14) and Stanford.

seconds in and a few moments later drew a foul on the center.

"It got us all excited," said Moore, who scored 21 of her game-high 34 points in the first half and had 12 rebounds to lead a 70-50 win.

All that stood in the path of an unprecedented second consecutive unbeaten season was Stanford. The Cardinal's only loss had been to UConn in Hartford on Dec. 23, and this would mark the third straight year the teams had met in the Final Four.

The championship game, certainly the first half, was UConn's blurriest in its remarkably clear two-year frame. The Huskies scored 12 points, the fewest ever scored in one half of a Final Four game. Still, they won 53-47, despite shooting only 32.8 percent (19-for-58), the lowest percentage by a winning team in an NCAA championship game.

"There was a point when I literally thought we might never score again," Auriemma said. "It was one of the few times I can ever remember being speechless. I've never seen anything like it."

The Huskies had their seventh national championship. They had a winning streak of 78. They had the Associated Press player of the year and Wooden Award winner (Charles) and the Wade Trophy winner (Moore).

"We force ourselves every day to do things that are against human nature," Moore said.

But more than anything, they had surpassed their own system of measure, one that all teams that follow likely will be hard-pressed to emulate.

How can anybody be better than perfect times two?

"We asked for this. We want to be great. We want to be the best team that we can be," Greene said. "We never said we wanted it to be easy."

BETTINA HANSEN

Fans watching on big screens back in Storrs cheer as the Huskies mount a comeback against Stanford in the final game.
After the game, an emotional Tina Charles, above, is joined by Chris Dailey and an array of fellow stars.

JOHN WOIKE

2012-2013 SEASON: 35-4

2013 NCAA TOURNAMENT: UConn 105, Idaho 37 • UConn 77, Vanderbilt 44 • **Sweet 16:** UConn 76, Maryland 50 •
Elite Eight: UConn 83, Kentucky 53 • **Semifinal:** UConn 83, Notre Dame 65 • **Final:** UConn 93, Louisville 60

Know Thy Enemy

I n ruby red stiletto heels and leather pencil skirt, Muffet McGraw brought high fashion to
the runway of women's college basketball long before the 2012-13 season.
   But as trailblazing as she was, it wasn't her sense of couture that diverted attention
from UConn as much as her plucky program at Notre Dame.
In the summer of 2007, Tennessee coach Pat Summitt, angered about recruiting tactics that
led Maya Moore to UConn, abruptly ended the illustrious series that had provided the sport
its most spirited rivalry and its growth chart since 1995.

Summitt's departure left the
stage open for a new central
character to star in the drama.
Was there another perceived
villainess willing to joust with
Geno Auriemma, the game's Prince
Valiant?

It turns out, there was. The
Fighting Irish had enhanced their
national recruiting and closed
the gap that separated UConn
from other schools even before

Happiness is meeting on the big stage
for Geno Auriemma and Notre Dame's
Muffet McGraw, two stylish coaches with
Philadelphia roots.
RICHARD MESSINA

ROSTER: Brianna Banks, Heather Buck, Stefanie Dolson, Caroline Doty, Kelly Faris, Bria Hartley, Moriah Jefferson,
Kaleena Mosqueda-Lewis, Breanna Stewart, Kiah Stokes, Morgan Tuck
COACHES: Geno Auriemma, Chris Dailey, Shea Ralph, Marisa Moseley

Stefanie Dolson, hooks Notre Dame's Kayla McBride in UConn's Final Four win in 2013, after there had been no holding back the Irish in three previous meetings that season.

CLOE POISSON

JOHN WOIKE

Aside from Notre Dame, Baylor is the only team against which the Huskies come up short, as Baylor's Brittney Griner scores 25 to beat UConn on Feb. 18, 2013 at the XL Center.

STEPHEN DUNN

Hampered at times by knee problems, freshman Morgan Tuck is at full speed against Rutgers, scoring 15 in a 65-45 victory.

BRAD HORRIGAN

Even with hands in her face, the shooting eye of Kaleena Mosqueda-Lewis rarely failed. She hit 49.2 percent of her threes, best in the nation.

that second consecutive unbeaten national championship in 2010.

"We keep talking about the Fighting Irish. We are the Fighting Irish. Let's give it a go," McGraw said.

Meanwhile, as Notre Dame brightened its rainbow, UConn endured a bittersweet two-year transition after its seventh national championship.

The Huskies said goodbye to Tina Charles in 2010 and then Moore, their first four-time All-American and career scoring leader (3,306). They also greeted a freshman class in 2010 highlighted by two kids from New York —

Stefanie Dolson, a flamboyant center from Port Jervis, N.Y., and Bria Hartley, an all-business guard from Long Island.

And they had done something truly remarkable, surpassing the 88-game winning streak of John Wooden's UCLA men in December 2010. They extended it to 90 at the start of a two-game California trip at Pacific on Dec. 28 before Stanford put a stop to it in a 12-point thumping in Palo Alto on Dec. 30.

Despite going 69-7, winning two Big East regular season championships and making it

MARK MIRKO

JOHN WOIKE

JOHN WOIKE:

During the regular season, Stefanie Dolson, top, brings the fire against Louisville; Bria Hartley, left, supplies the acrobatics against Pitt, helping get the Huskies to Bridgeport, where freshman Moriah Jefferson, above right, looks for a way around Maryland in the Sweet 16.

Above left, Brittany Mallory (22) celebrates against UConn in the 2011 national semifinals, beginning a 7-1 Notre Dame run in the series. But, in 2014, when Muffet McGraw stalks the sideline in the title game against the Huskies, the Irish are down on their luck.

A year earlier UConn's season ends in the Final Four against Notre Dame – but this one in overtime, just adding to the misery for Stefanie Dolson (31), Kaleena Mosqueda-Lewis (23) and Caroline Doty.

In South Bend, the 2012-13 regular season is extended by three overtimes, and Notre Dame wins 96-87 despite five blocks by UConn freshman Breanna Stewart, right.

to the Final Four, the Huskies were not able to win a national championship in either year. Although it was Texas A&M and Baylor that won, it was clear to anyone keeping score who really was responsible for stunting UConn's growth.

McGraw arrived in South Bend, Ind., in 1995 and lost her first 11 games against Auriemma before a 16-point win on her campus on Jan. 15, 2001. Three months later, in the national semifinal in St. Louis when Diana Taurasi's compass failed, the Irish beat UConn on the way to their first national championship.

But it really wasn't until April 2011 that it became clear, at least to UConn, that an opponent had arrived not only willing to stare

it down, but capable of beating it down.

On April 3, 2011, after rolling off 24 wins following the end of their 90-game streak, and already beating Notre Dame three times, the Huskies lost to the Irish 72-63 in the national semifinals in Indianapolis. It was just the fourth loss in Moore's illustrious 154-game run.

"If the other team is lousy, it's not a problem playing them four times," Auriemma said. "You wish you could play them 12 times. But playing a really good team for the fourth time is ideally not something you want to be doing."

Playing, even with a sprained foot, Kelly Faris has 21 points and 13 rebounds in 53 minutes in the triple-OT loss, while Skylar Diggins scores 29 for the Irish.

CLOE POISSON

The Irish then beat UConn three of four the next season, the third in Denver, in overtime, in another national semifinal.

"Once we beat them in the Final Four it was an eye-opener for us," Notre Dame's Brittany Mallory said. "We could play with them; we had as many good players. ... We realized we weren't playing anyone special, just another team."

But in 2012, three more game-changers arrived in Storrs. There was Texas guard Moriah Jefferson, Illinois post Morgan Tuck and Breanna Stewart from Syracuse, N.Y. Stewart was the one with an expansive wingspan and an extraordinary talent that some compare to NBA great Kevin Durant.

By then, Hartley and Dolson were juniors. And the Big East freshman of the year the previous season had been Kaleena Mosqueda-Lewis, a phenomenal shooter. Kelly Faris, a senior, was the best all-around fundamental player on the team.

Enough of the blues against Notre Dame: UConn supporters jazz up their outfits at the 2013 Final Four in New Orleans, above, and Breanna Stewart, left, has 29 points to push Ariel Braker and the Irish out of the picture.

CLOE POISSON

High-flying Caroline Doty and her teammates don't have to sweat out the finish against Notre Dame this time, winning by 18 in the 2013 NCAA semifinals. From far right: Kiah Stokes, Moriah Jefferson and Kaleena Mosqueda-Lewis.
CLOE POISSON

The Cards seem stacked against her, but Stefanie Dolson beats Louisville to a rebound in the championship game.
CLOE POISSON

"I'm hoping that [the freshmen] keep getting better and better and that when I look back at the end of the year I will be able to say that they can have that kind of immediate impact," Auriemma said.

And they did, sort of. Tuck was injured, Jefferson was prone to inconsistency, and Hartley struggled with an ankle injury sustained the previous summer playing for USA Basketball. But Stewart was sensational, and Mosqueda-Lewis drained a program-record 118 three-pointers.

Still, Notre Dame continued to be a nemesis. UConn finished 35-4, but three of the defeats were to the Irish: a one-point loss at Gampel Pavilion in January; a three-overtime loss in the regular season finale at South Bend during which Faris injured her foot; and a crushing two-point loss in the final Big East Tournament championship game in Hartford.

Astonishingly, Notre Dame had won four in a row and seven of eight against UConn as the NCAA Tournament began.

And for the 12th time in the past three seasons, it was Notre Dame waiting again in the national semifinal.

But this time Stewart, who would be the Final Four's most outstanding player, scored 29 points to fuel an 83-65 win. That victory in New Orleans paved the path to UConn's eighth national championship, which the Huskies won by 33 points two nights later against Louisville.

Notre Dame and McGraw were sent packing — at least until the following April, as it turned out.

You can tell by the Huskies' expressions that the final is going well, as Breanna Stewart, second from right, draws a foul.
CLOE POISSON

CLOE POISSON

What a way to end a career for Kelly Faris, above, who played 154 games for Geno Auriemma, contributing 16 points, nine rebounds and six assists in her finale. Back home the next day, from left, Moriah Jefferson, Stefanie Dolson, Morgan Tuck and Breanna Stewart help conduct a campus tour for a shiny new arrival.

MARK MIRKO

2013-2014 SEASON: 40-0

2014 NCAA TOURNAMENT: UConn 87, Prairie View A&M 44 • UConn 91, St. Joseph's 52 • **Sweet 16:** UConn 70, BYU 51 •
Elite Eight: UConn 69, Texas A&M 54 • **Semifinals:** UConn 75, Stanford 56 • **Final:** UConn 79, Notre Dame 58

American Experience

U Conn's athletic department was essentially born in the late 1940s in a place called the Yankee Conference. If you look on the walls of Hugh Greer Field House, you can still see the family pictures, taken in pastoral New England settings such as Burlington, Vt., and Durham, N.H.
In the autumn and winter, they played football and basketball, and athletic directors asked about each other's kids. Everybody was connected.

The Huskies could have stayed in the Yankee Conference forever, if forever had been an option. But in 1979, a high-rise called the Big East Conference was built in Providence by a dreamer named Dave Gavitt.

Gavitt was interested in expanding the focus of sports in New England beyond established provincial borders. And he invited UConn to lease basketball space.

When you go undefeated, there are very few reasons to get down on yourself. Kaleena Mosqueda-Lewis playfully ducks under the trophy after the AAC title game in March.
CLOE POISSON

ROSTER: Brianna Banks, Saniya Chong, Stefanie Dolson, Bria Hartley, Moriah Jefferson, Tierney Lawlor, Kaleena Mosqueda-Lewis, Briana Pulido, Breanna Stewart, Kiah Stokes, Morgan Tuck
COACHES: Geno Auriemma, Chris Dailey, Shea Ralph, Marisa Moseley

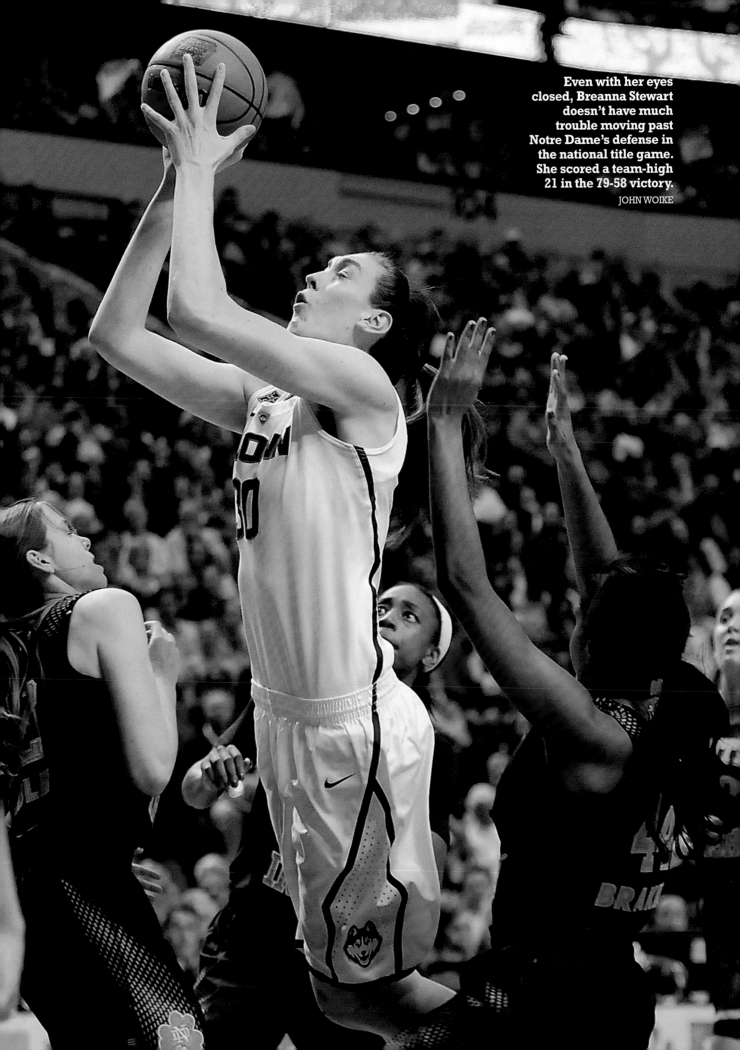

Even with her eyes closed, Breanna Stewart doesn't have much trouble moving past Notre Dame's defense in the national title game. She scored a team-high 21 in the 79-58 victory.
JOHN WOIKE

Look back at the stat sheet and you'll see sophomore Moriah Jefferson led the Huskies in assists (195) and steals (106) and was second in three-point percentage (41.8) in the 2013-14 season.
CLOE POISSON

JOHN WOIKE

Saniya Chong, reaching for a loose ball against Memphis in January, earned a spot on the AAC all-freshman team. She played in 39 of 40 games, in the 2013-14 season, and shot 82.5 percent from the free-throw line, second-best on the team.

Finally, though not without hesitation, the Huskies said yes.

This bold choice served UConn well. The Big East incubated the most inspiring women's basketball program in the nation. As it turned out, the UConn women won eight national championships while in the league.

By 2013, you watched "Bonanza" reruns on a phone and college football bowl games on a flat-screen TV. And then everything changed. The cash and influence from football shook up UConn's world.

Some schools in the Big East, including UConn, decided money and football mattered more than basketball and left for other conferences.

Geno Auriemma found his

Breanna Stewart foils Temple center Taylor Robinson, who shot just 3-for-13 in UConn's 80-36 rout Jan. 11, 2014, in Bridgeport.

BRAD HORRIGAN

CLOE POISSON

The senior leadership of Bria Hartley helped UConn get a handle on distractions all season. She had 17 points and five assists against Louisville in the AAC title game.

program in the American Athletic Conference at the start of 2013-14 season. He didn't have to deal with Notre Dame anymore. The Fighting Irish had joined the Atlantic Coast Conference. He didn't have Kelly Faris, either. His indestructible defender with a steel jaw to match her resolve had gone to the WNBA's Connecticut Sun.

What he did have were charter flights to Houston and Dallas, Florida golf dates in Orlando and Tampa, and a blend of All-America talent in sophomore Breanna Stewart, junior Kaleena Mosqueda-Lewis and seniors Stefanie Dolson and Bria Hartley.

"It's kind of exciting for me, to be honest," Auriemma said. "We don't know anything about each other — opponents' tendencies. I've never even been in many of the gymnasiums we'll visit."

As it turned out, AAC opponents fell in sequential order. UConn won 18 conference games by an average

JOHN WOIKE

Kaleena Mosqueda-Lewis is helped to her feet after a scary fall in the Nov. 11 win over Stanford. She missed eight games because of the elbow injury.

of 37.5 points, holding opponents to just 44.9 points and a shooting percentage of 28.9 percent.

UConn's nonconference schedule proved equally solvable. Third-ranked Stanford fell by

19 points at Gampel Pavilion in November 2013 and a week later No. 8 Maryland and No. 13 Penn State followed on the road by a combined 36 points. The Huskies embarrassed No. 2 Duke by 22 at Cameron Indoor Stadium just before Christmas.

During the course of a 31-game regular season, only Baylor, which fell by 11 in Waco, Texas, on Jan. 13, 2014, offered a real scare. With 10:54 to play, UConn's lead was 50-49.

UConn's problems were of a different kind.

In that Stanford game, Mosqueda-Lewis, who had set the program's single-season record with 118 three-pointers in an All-America sophomore season, fell hard on her elbow causing damage to her ulnar nerve. She screamed so loudly it sent chills to the top rows of Gampel Pavilion.

"Help me!" Mosqueda-Lewis yelled. "Help me!"

She would miss eight games

Sometimes it seems like nothing rattles Kaleena Mosqueda-Lewis. Despite the Cameron Crazies trying to put a hex on her, the affable junior scored 21 points, all on threes, in UConn's 83-61 win at Duke on Dec. 17. It was her first game back from injury.

before returning with seven threes in the win at Duke. And just before the game at South Florida on Feb. 16, UConn announced she had mononucleosis. She missed four more.

Morgan Tuck, the quiet and resourceful sophomore post from Illinois, had greater problems. After fighting through a left knee injury as a freshman, she eventually succumbed, but not before scoring 19 points and shooting 8-for-10 in a win over Houston on Jan. 7. She then had season-ending knee surgery.

So it was left to Stewart, the most outstanding player in the 2013 Final Four, to step forward. And it was left to Hartley, the kid from

Things are looking up on New Year's Day 2014 when Morgan Tuck and the Huskies outmuscle Central Florida 77-49 to run their record to 15-0.

The eyes have it: Breanna Stewart, Kaleena Mosqueda-Lewis and Stefanie Dolson goof around during a promo for ESPN before the Final Four in Nashville. The Huskies saw so clearly that they beat Stanford and Notre Dame by a combined 40 points.

JOHN WOIKE

UConn uses a powerful ground game to beat Stanford and All-America forward Chiney Ogwumike 75-56 in the 2014 national semifinal. Kiah Stokes, left, was 4-for-4 from the floor.

Long Island who originally wanted to play lacrosse, and Dolson, the free spirit from Port Jervis, N.Y., who transformed her body into a working machine two years earlier, to push aside what opposition there was.

The Huskies won their first AAC title with a 20-point victory over Louisville, then sailed through NCAA wins that led to another — and this time historic — meeting with Notre Dame in the NCAA championship game in Nashville.

For the first time, two undefeated teams would play for the NCAA title. But this was not the 1960s anymore. Notre Dame's Muffet McGraw was in no mood to lend UConn a cup of sugar. Since UConn's loss to the Irish in the 2011 national semifinals, Notre Dame had won seven of the past nine,

With Breanna Stewart scoring 18 points and Kaleena Mosqueda-Lewis 15, Stanford rarely focused on Bria Hartley (14) in the Final Four. The senior finished with 13 points and four assists.

The mouth that roared: Emotional team leader, No. 1 cheerleader and fan favorite Stefanie Dolson makes sure everybody in Nashville knows UConn is having no trouble with Notre Dame in the championship game.

JOHN WOIKE

It's always a banner day when UConn and Notre Dame meet, but it intensifies when a championship is at stake — the first between two undefeated teams. Bridgestone Arena in Nashville was the site of the Huskies' ninth title on April 8, 2014.

including three of four in 2012-13.

On the day before the title game, McGraw was asked about the perception the programs didn't like each other, and whether the coaches could regain civility.

"I think we're past the point," she said.

Auriemma did not back down.

"Why is she angry? I don't know. You have to ask her. I haven't changed in 25 years," Auriemma said. "People that know me understand I haven't changed. How I run my program hasn't changed, the respect we have for everyone

Short stop: Just 5 feet 7, Moriah Jefferson (4) is a persistent pest, stealing the ball from Notre Dame's Kayla McBride, foreground, in the Huskies' 79-58 victory.

else hasn't changed.

"We think we are the best basketball team in the country, but we don't flaunt it. But a funny thing happens to people once they start beating us."

Notre Dame did not beat UConn on April 8, 2014. The Huskies, for the first time, went 40-0 and won their ninth national championship in a 79-58 rout that capped the college careers of Dolson and Hartley in All-America laurel. Stewart again was national player of the year.

In The American, UConn might have been in a different home, a neighborhood where it was more trouble to get around. But boy, the sofa was just as comfortable.

Geno Auriemma realizes the Huskies' ninth title is within his grasp, above, and Brianna Banks shows the world how a national champ dances on a confetti-laden floor.

JOHN WOIKE

JOHN WOIKE

2014-2015 SEASON: 38-1

2015 NCAA TOURNAMENT: UConn 89, St. Francis Brooklyn 33 • UConn 91, Rutgers 55 • **Sweet 16:** UConn 105, Texas 54 •
Elite Eight: UConn 91, Dayton 70 • **Semifinal:** UConn 81, Maryland 58 • **Final:** UConn 63, Notre Dame 53

Sustained Greatness

B y the time John Thurston brought St. Francis Brooklyn to Gampel Pavilion in March 2015 to play its first-ever NCAA Tournament game, the silver-haired man with a distinctive New York lilt was well into his fifth decade coaching men's and women's basketball.

The day before his Terriers played No. 1 UConn, which had careened through its second season in the American Athletic Conference like a twister across the flatland, Thurston was asked what it felt like to be the biggest underdog in either NCAA Tournament.

"You know, a lot of people root for underdogs," Thurston said. "But I have always been intrigued by those who are able to maintain a dynasty. That is so much harder. You can pop your head up once in a while, but to maintain excellence at the highest level is so incredibly difficult to do. I really admire those people.

"The only thing I can compare UConn to in the time I have been

UConn players put on their party faces to celebrate Geno Auriemma's 900th win, against Cincinnati on Feb. 3, an occasion where Chris Dailey also laughs at herself.
JOHN WOIKE

ROSTER: Natalie Butler, Saniya Chong, Sadie Edwards, Courtney Ekmark, Moriah Jefferson, Tierney Lawlor, Kaleena Mosqueda-Lewis, Kia Nurse, Briana Pulido, Breanna Stewart, Kiah Stokes, Morgan Tuck, Gabby Williams
COACHES: Geno Auriemma, Chris Dailey, Shea Ralph, Marisa Moseley

Geno Auriemma's 100th
NCAA Tournament win,
against Texas in the
Sweet 16, isn't much of
a test, and he's already
looking ahead.

CLOE POISSON

It's Kaleena Mosqueda-Lewis, left, vs. Notre Dame's Michaela Mabrey in UConn's 76-58 Jimmy V Classic win on Dec. 6, 2014, in South Bend.

around is UCLA. I haven't seen anything else quite like it in my experience — the sustained excellence. I don't know if it can ever be duplicated. It's astonishing to see, sitting where I am."

Geno Auriemma's program frequently has been compared to the UCLA men, coached by John Wooden, the Wizard of Westwood, since the night in Hartford — Dec. 21, 2010 — when Maya Moore scored a career-high 41 points to lead UConn to its 89th consecutive victory.

That was one more than the record run Wooden's team compiled in the 1960s and 1970s, when the Bruins were redefining dynasty by winning 10 national championships in 12 seasons.

And from that point on it

Only Stanford sent UConn off the court with a loss – 88-86 in overtime on Nov. 17, 2014 – but for Kiah Stokes and the Huskies, there was no looking back.

appeared even clearer that Auriemma was an icon in his own right, closing in on another, but with the advantage of youth and time on his side.

So, on a 46-game winning streak, with their sparkling new Werth Champions Center and five freshmen to replenish the loss of two All-Americans, Stefanie Dolson and Bria Hartley, the Huskies opened the 2014-15 season with a big win at UC Davis and big goals. They were aiming for a third straight national championship and a 10th for Auriemma. That would tie him with the great Wooden for the most in history.

Junior Breanna Stewart, the reigning national player of the year, and senior Kaleena Mosqueda-Lewis would have to

UConn center Kiah Stokes, left, swivels away as East Carolina doubles up the pressure in the American Athletic Conference tournament semifinal at Mohegan Sun on March 7, which the Huskies won decisively, 106-56.

Studying an opponent is one way to prepare for a game, but assistant coach Shea Ralph, left, shows Kia Nurse another way to try to influence the outcome at the NCAA regional in Albany.

When Tiffany Mitchell (25) overshoots her landing,
it's all UConn around the basket, and Moriah
Jefferson drives in an 87-62 rout of then-No. 1 South
Carolina on Feb. 9, 2015, in Storrs.
JOHN WOIKE

The Gampel career of Kaleena Mosqueda-Lewis, center, ends in an NCAA second-round win over Rutgers, in which she had a game-high 23 points. It's a moment that Morgan Tuck, left, and Moriah Jefferson clearly enjoy sharing.

lead.

Strong contributions would have to come from junior point guard Moriah Jefferson and forward Morgan Tuck, whose previous season ended with knee surgery.

Senior center Kiah Stokes, blessed with a strong athletic frame, would need to play with more mental toughness and consistency. And how would the freshmen contribute, especially Canadian guard Kia Nurse, whose springboard to Storrs was her summer as the youngest member of her nation's senior national team at the FIBA World Cup in Turkey?

Brady Sanders of Texas fouls Kia Nurse, left, in the Sweet 16, but the UConn machine isn't susceptible to hacking; the Huskies shut down the Longhorns, 105-54.

As it turned out, the result far exceeded expectations, even after Stanford, which had ended UConn's 90-game streak in 2010, then offered a curtain call in November when it snapped the Huskies' 47-game winning streak in Palo Alto by two points in overtime.

The loss might have been the best thing that could have happened to the Huskies, particularly after their 40-0 record the year before. Auriemma had the team's attention and jumped at the chance to prove a point. He inserted Tuck and Nurse into the starting lineup. And immediately, assertively, UConn began to roll, winning its home opener against Creighton by 36 points.

On Dec. 6, Tuck scored 25 points, Stokes had 18 rebounds, and UConn smashed Notre Dame 76-58 in South Bend, in the renewal of their regular season series. Before New Year's, DePaul, UCLA and

MICHAEL McANDREWS

Geno Auriemma congratulates Kaleena Mosqueda-Lewis, who hit seven three-pointers against Dayton to surpass the NCAA career record of 392.

With Dayton posing a threat in the first half, Breanna Stewart (30) is in an expansive mood after halftime as she boxes out Ally Malott, with help from Kia Nurse.

CLOE POISSON

Duke also were easily dismissed.

One of the five freshmen, Sadie Edwards, who began her high school career playing for state power Mercy-Middletown, transferred to the University of Southern California. UConn hardly missed a beat. Jefferson was flying around the floor and conference teams began falling. Stokes and Mosqueda-Lewis grew closer to program and national records for blocked shots and made three-pointers.

On Feb. 9 at Gampel Pavilion, in the midst of a nasty snow, the Huskies demolished No. 1 South Carolina by 25 points, with Mosqueda-Lewis (23 points) and Stewart (22) leading the way. And on March 2 in Tampa, the Huskies

CLOE POISSON

Maryland coach Brenda Frese's pregame preparations at the Final Four don't go as planned.

ended the regular season 29-1 with a 23-point win over South Florida. UConn went 18-0 in the AAC.

Auriemma also became the all-time winningest coach in women's basketball and just the

sixth women's coach to win 900 games. Stokes, who rarely took a shot, broke Rebecca Lobo's record for most blocked shots in a season (131) with emphatic force.

And in UConn's Elite Eight win over Dayton in Albany on March 30, after trailing at halftime for the first time in 83 games — dating to March 12, 2013 — Mosqueda-Lewis set the NCAA record for most career three-pointers. She made seven in the stirring 91-70 victory that sent the Huskies to an eighth consecutive Final Four.

By the time the Huskies played Maryland in the semifinals in Tampa, Fla., Stewart had been handed the Wade Trophy and awarded her second national player of the year award by

CLOE POISSON

Morgan Tuck, driving against Shatori Walker-Kimbrough (32), steps into the national spotlight in the April 5, 2105, semifinal with 24 points and nine rebounds – one shy of a double-double.

Undeterred by Notre Dame's Lindsay Allen (15), Moriah Jefferson shoots during the second half of the April 7 championship game in Tampa. Jefferson had 15 points, including three three-pointers.

CLOE POISSON

CLOE POISSON

The UConn women rejoice after defeating Notre Dame, 63-53, to win the NCAA final and the Huskies' 10th national championship at Amalie Arena in Tampa on April 7.

The Associated Press. Stewart, Mosqueda-Lewis and Jefferson were honored as WBCA first-team All-Americans.

"I mean, aren't we tired of it?" Maryland coach Brenda Frese said of UConn's dominance. "I think everyone is rooting for us. I think we are ready for some new stories. And our sport needs it, to be quite honest."

If hearing that wasn't enough to stoke the Huskies, they also had watched Kentucky's undefeated men's team, considered by some to be unbeatable, lose its semifinal to Wisconsin. So on April 5, led by Stewart (25 points, eight rebounds) and Tuck (24 points, nine rebounds), the Huskies easily sailed to another championship game with a breezy 81-58 win.

There waiting – again, of course – was Notre Dame, which had squeaked by South Carolina by a point on a basket by Madison Cable with 13.9 seconds to play.

And although it wasn't easy, especially after Stewart twisted her ankle in the first half, the Huskies

managed to do what they've seemingly always managed to do. On a very difficult night, when all did not go right, they defeated the Irish, 63-53.

UConn finished the season 38-1, on a 37-game winning streak with 18 consecutive NCAA Tournament victories tucked in its championship belt. Stewart (eight points, 15 rebounds) was named most outstanding player of the Final Four for the third consecutive year, an achievement accomplished only by Kareem

Abdul-Jabbar when he was still known as Lew Alcindor at UCLA.

"I said I wanted to win four [championships]," Stewart said. "You can't win four without winning three."

Auriemma, at that point tied historically to Wooden and the NBA's Phil Jackson, who won 10 titles with the Bulls and the Lakers, was overjoyed.

"This is an incredible group. ... Every day this team just kept working and working. They deserve everything."

Yes, sustained greatness — UConn's hallmark through the past 20 seasons and 10 national championships. To some, that is the most impressive accomplishment in this castle in the cornfield that Geno Auriemma and Chris Dailey and the greatest players in the modern era of women's basketball have built.

MICHAEL McANDREWS

Record-breaking shooter Kaleena Mosqueda-Lewis flexes her defense as well in the title game's second half.

MICHAEL McANDREWS

A bit of net holds buckets of memories for three-time Most Outstanding Player Breanna Stewart.

Kaleena Mosqueda-Lewis, whose late-game pair of three-pointers widened UConn's edge, hoists the NCAA championship trophy, with teammates including, from left, Morgan Tuck, Saniya Chong and Moriah Jefferson.

CLOE POISSON

What Makes Geno Tick?

Ten.

The number screams Wooden. Only John Wooden never screamed. Ten.

"I am not John Wooden," Geno Auriemma said softly at the start of the 2015 NCAA Tournament.

No. 1 for Auriemma arrived in another century, on a basketball court in Minneapolis, against a coach who everyone seemed to agree would amass victories and national championships that never would be surpassed.

But Auriemma surpassed Tennessee's Pat Summitt with No. 9 in 2014 on a Nashville basketball

court in a national championship collision of unbeaten teams for the first time in either men's or women's history.

This particular collision was against Notre Dame and Muffet McGraw, but in truth there always seems to be a collision for Auriemma. Whether it's vs. Tennessee or Notre Dame … or Geno's Frankie Avalon hair vs. Baylor coach Kim Mulkey's sparkly outfits … or Auriemma's acerbic tongue vs. the Cameron Crazies' craziness … yes, there is always some kind of collision and it's usually noisy.

Not with Auriemma's 10th

national title on a basketball court in Tampa, Fla. Not with the national title that matches Wooden's legendary total with the UCLA men spanning 1964-1975. Not with Ten.

"Do I mind [being compared to Wooden]?" Auriemma said. "Well, it's better than being compared to what I used to be compared to when I started coaching or the shock when we ever lose a game now."

Stop right there. Wise guy alert!

Wooden said things that could be carved into eternity, things such as, "Talent is God-given. Be humble. Fame is man-given. Be grateful. Conceit is self-given. Be careful." Auriemma says things that can be posted on a school's student union bulletin board, things such as, "There are just as many Duke graduates waiting on tables as ... from any other school in the country. They may just be working at a better restaurant."

In the end, we are products of our upbringing. Wooden was a Midwest boy from the early 20th century who moved to Los Angeles yet never lost his Midwestern principles and sensibilities. He was the only humble man left in Hollywood. Luigi Auriemma may have immigrated to America with his family when he was 7, but he unmistakably is the product of Philly and Philly basketball. Sharp of mind, sharp of tongue.

Wooden's idea of profanity was, "Gracious sakes alive." Auriemma's idea of profanity? Let's just say it isn't goodness sakes alive.

No. 2 for Auriemma fittingly came in Philly in 2000 when he ran a back-door play so many times on Summitt, he flat ran Tennessee out of his hometown. Nos. 3, 4 and 5 arrived in short order, marked by Auriemma's greatest team in 2002 with Swin Cash, Sue Bird, Asjha Jones and continued with one letter — D — for the next two. D as in Auriemma famously saying, "We have Diana Taurasi and you don't."

Nos. 6 and 7 arrived with the majesty of Maya Moore and Tina Charles. Nos. 8, 9 and 10 with Breanna Stewart and Kaleena Mosqueda-Lewis, and if you see the great names in women's basketball mounting here, that is no mistake. Wooden had Walton, Alcindor, Goodrich, Wilkes, Wicks, etc. As Wooden once said, he'd take a lot of talent and little experience any day over a little talent.

Ten. Make no mistake it took overwhelming talent.

"UCLA's freshman team one year beat their national champions with almost everybody back," Auriemma said, referring to the Pauley Pavilion opening game in November 1965. "That's how many good players they had in their program at one point. Up until recently, women's basketball had a few teams with all the best players. Now, it's kind of spread out a little bit more. There are a lot more good teams, not as many great teams. So we're in a similar era to UCLA when their dynasty was in full force."

As a young guy, Auriemma loved the Bruins of the 1960s. He loved their talent and precision. Those powder blue and gold uniforms were classic. Above all, he came to idolize their coach. Even as the Huskies were on the road toward UCLA's record of 88 consecutive victories — breaking it in 2010 only months after Wooden's death at 99 — Auriemma carried one of Wooden's books in his briefcase. The day Wooden died I called Auriemma and his first words were telling. He thanked me for a chance to comment on a man he idolized.

The two met once. It was in California in the 1990s. Wooden was appearing at a clinic. Auriemma was awestruck. He has said it was like meeting Babe Ruth. Auriemma can fill a room with stories, but he did the listening that night. A number of years later in the midst of the Huskies' first three-peat, Wooden wrote glowingly in Sports Illustrated about the way the UConn women played and how it reminded him of his UCLA teams but noted he had not met their pleasant young coach.

Over the years, Auriemma has come to laugh about that. He figures Wooden, the ultimate teacher, was sending him a subliminal message about humility. If John Wooden doesn't remember, then you're still a nobody.

"Winning in women's college basketball is a lot harder than it was 20 years ago," Auriemma said. "But I never competed against John Wooden. I never competed against any of the people he competed against. I don't live in that arena. I'm not comfortable being compared to people in that world. It's a completely different world, even though it's the same game, it's not.

"I think they should keep it separate. I don't think Coach K is waking up saying, 'I need five more to catch Geno.' I don't think Serena Williams' goal was to catch Pete Sampras. You compete against the people you compete against, and I'd just like to leave it at that."

Yet to leave it at that is also to miss the essence of what brought both men to Ten. The mistake, I've long felt, is trying to force an intersection of the two men and their great programs. The sublime appreciation is in treasuring the parallel paths. They both chased perfection each and every day, totally immersed in playing the game the right way. One did it in a crisply tailored way with a Pyramid of Success. The other has sometimes done it by the seat of his pants.

Auriemma has insisted there is one thing under-appreciated about Wooden. Something buried in all the focus on Wooden's wonderful philosophies and legendary discipline. He marvels at the way Wooden got great players to work together, to move without the ball, to treasure sharing it, to accept sitting on the bench until it was their turn to shine.

"Getting great players to submit totally to winning," Auriemma told me in 2010. "John Wooden was the master of it."

At Ten and counting, the same could be said of Geno Auriemma.

– Jeff Jacobs

Victory over Tennessee is sweet for UConn coach Geno Auriemma, as the 2000 NCAA champion Huskies carry him off the court in his hometown of Philadelphia.

MICHAEL McANDREWS

The 63-53 victory over Notre Dame was anything
but easy, but netting the Huskies' 10th NCAA title
is a jubilant high for coach Geno Auriemma.
MICHAEL McANDREWS